Large Print Color by Numbers for Adults:

Wild Animal Kingdom

COLORING TEST PAGE

COLORING TEST PAGE

Welcome to the *Large Print Color by Numbers for Adults: Wild Animal Kingdom.* This beautiful activity book features a coloring key on the left page and artwork on the right.

Color by number books are a great way to relieve stress, relax and help you mind focus. The best part? Even though this was designed for adults, this activity is fun for **all ages!** Color with the kids, mom, dad or even grandma and grandpa.

We hope you enjoy this coloring activity book. We look forward to hearing your feedback on ***Amazon!***

Key Colors:

1. Red
2. Green
3. Yellow
4. Blue
5. Orange
6. Purple
7. Cyan
8. Magenta
9. Lime
10. Pink
11. Teal
12. Lavender
13. Brown
14. Beige
15. Maroon
16. Mint
17. Olive
18. Coral
19. Navy
20. Grey
21. White
22. Black
23. Silver
24. Sky Blue
25. Colbalt Green
26. Gold
27. Gingerbread
28. Olive
29. Turquoise
30. Peach

Key Colors:

1. Red	16. Mint
2. Green	17. Olive
3. Yellow	18. Coral
4. Blue	19. Navy
5. Orange	20. Grey
6. Purple	21. White
7. Cyan	22. Black
8. Magenta	23. Silver
9. Lime	24. Sky Blue
10. Pink	25. Colbalt Green
11. Teal	26. Gold
12. Lavender	27. Gingerbread
13. Brown	28. Olive
14. Beige	29. Turquoise
15. Maroon	30. Peach

Key Colors:

1. Red
2. Green
3. Yellow
4. Blue
5. Orange
6. Purple
7. Cyan
8. Magenta
9. Lime
10. Pink
11. Teal
12. Lavender
13. Brown
14. Beige
15. Maroon
16. Mint
17. Olive
18. Coral
19. Navy
20. Grey
21. White
22. Black
23. Silver
24. Sky Blue
25. Colbalt Green
26. Gold
27. Gingerbread
28. Olive
29. Turquoise
30. Peach

Key Colors:

1. Red
2. Green
3. Yellow
4. Blue
5. Orange
6. Purple
7. Cyan
8. Magenta
9. Lime
10. Pink
11. Teal
12. Lavender
13. Brown
14. Beige
15. Maroon
16. Mint
17. Olive
18. Coral
19. Navy
20. Grey
21. White
22. Black
23. Silver
24. Sky Blue
25. Colbalt Green
26. Gold
27. Gingerbread
28. Olive
29. Turquoise
30. Peach

24
20
16
20
16
16
13
13
16
2
14
2
11
13
13
13
11
11
14
14
14
14
14
28
17
17
14

Key Colors:

1. Red
2. Green
3. Yellow
4. Blue
5. Orange
6. Purple
7. Cyan
8. Magenta
9. Lime
10. Pink
11. Teal
12. Lavender
13. Brown
14. Beige
15. Maroon
16. Mint
17. Olive
18. Coral
19. Navy
20. Grey
21. White
22. Black
23. Silver
24. Sky Blue
25. Colbalt Green
26. Gold
27. Gingerbread
28. Olive
29. Turquoise
30. Peach

Key Colors:

1. Red	16. Mint
2. Green	17. Olive
3. Yellow	18. Coral
4. Blue	19. Navy
5. Orange	20. Grey
6. Purple	21. White
7. Cyan	22. Black
8. Magenta	23. Silver
9. Lime	24. Sky Blue
10. Pink	25. Colbalt Green
11. Teal	26. Gold
12. Lavender	27. Gingerbread
13. Brown	28. Olive
14. Beige	29. Turquoise
15. Maroon	30. Peach

Key Colors:

1. Red
2. Green
3. Yellow
4. Blue
5. Orange
6. Purple
7. Cyan
8. Magenta
9. Lime
10. Pink
11. Teal
12. Lavender
13. Brown
14. Beige
15. Maroon
16. Mint
17. Olive
18. Coral
19. Navy
20. Grey
21. White
22. Black
23. Silver
24. Sky Blue
25. Colbalt Green
26. Gold
27. Gingerbread
28. Olive
29. Turquoise
30. Peach

Key Colors:

1. Red
2. Green
3. Yellow
4. Blue
5. Orange
6. Purple
7. Cyan
8. Magenta
9. Lime
10. Pink
11. Teal
12. Lavender
13. Brown
14. Beige
15. Maroon
16. Mint
17. Olive
18. Coral
19. Navy
20. Grey
21. White
22. Black
23. Silver
24. Sky Blue
25. Colbalt Green
26. Gold
27. Gingerbread
28. Olive
29. Turquoise
30. Peach

Key Colors:

1. Red	16. Mint
2. Green	17. Olive
3. Yellow	18. Coral
4. Blue	19. Navy
5. Orange	20. Grey
6. Purple	21. White
7. Cyan	22. Black
8. Magenta	23. Silver
9. Lime	24. Sky Blue
10. Pink	25. Colbalt Green
11. Teal	26. Gold
12. Lavender	27. Gingerbread
13. Brown	28. Olive
14. Beige	29. Turquoise
15. Maroon	30. Peach

Key Colors:

1. Red
2. Green
3. Yellow
4. Blue
5. Orange
6. Purple
7. Cyan
8. Magenta
9. Lime
10. Pink
11. Teal
12. Lavender
13. Brown
14. Beige
15. Maroon
16. Mint
17. Olive
18. Coral
19. Navy
20. Grey
21. White
22. Black
23. Silver
24. Sky Blue
25. Colbalt Green
26. Gold
27. Gingerbread
28. Olive
29. Turquoise
30. Peach

Key Colors:

1. Red
2. Green
3. Yellow
4. Blue
5. Orange
6. Purple
7. Cyan
8. Magenta
9. Lime
10. Pink
11. Teal
12. Lavender
13. Brown
14. Beige
15. Maroon
16. Mint
17. Olive
18. Coral
19. Navy
20. Grey
21. White
22. Black
23. Silver
24. Sky Blue
25. Colbalt Green
26. Gold
27. Gingerbread
28. Olive
29. Turquoise
30. Peach

Key Colors:

1. Red	16. Mint
2. Green	17. Olive
3. Yellow	18. Coral
4. Blue	19. Navy
5. Orange	20. Grey
6. Purple	21. White
7. Cyan	22. Black
8. Magenta	23. Silver
9. Lime	24. Sky Blue
10. Pink	25. Colbalt Green
11. Teal	26. Gold
12. Lavender	27. Gingerbread
13. Brown	28. Olive
14. Beige	29. Turquoise
15. Maroon	30. Peach

Key Colors:

1. Red
2. Green
3. Yellow
4. Blue
5. Orange
6. Purple
7. Cyan
8. Magenta
9. Lime
10. Pink
11. Teal
12. Lavender
13. Brown
14. Beige
15. Maroon
16. Mint
17. Olive
18. Coral
19. Navy
20. Grey
21. White
22. Black
23. Silver
24. Sky Blue
25. Colbalt Green
26. Gold
27. Gingerbread
28. Olive
29. Turquoise
30. Peach

Key Colors:

1. Red
2. Green
3. Yellow
4. Blue
5. Orange
6. Purple
7. Cyan
8. Magenta
9. Lime
10. Pink
11. Teal
12. Lavender
13. Brown
14. Beige
15. Maroon
16. Mint
17. Olive
18. Coral
19. Navy
20. Grey
21. White
22. Black
23. Silver
24. Sky Blue
25. Colbalt Green
26. Gold
27. Gingerbread
28. Olive
29. Turquoise
30. Peach

Key Colors:

1. Red
2. Green
3. Yellow
4. Blue
5. Orange
6. Purple
7. Cyan
8. Magenta
9. Lime
10. Pink
11. Teal
12. Lavender
13. Brown
14. Beige
15. Maroon
16. Mint
17. Olive
18. Coral
19. Navy
20. Grey
21. White
22. Black
23. Silver
24. Sky Blue
25. Colbalt Green
26. Gold
27. Gingerbread
28. Olive
29. Turquoise
30. Peach

Key Colors:

1. Red
2. Green
3. Yellow
4. Blue
5. Orange
6. Purple
7. Cyan
8. Magenta
9. Lime
10. Pink
11. Teal
12. Lavender
13. Brown
14. Beige
15. Maroon
16. Mint
17. Olive
18. Coral
19. Navy
20. Grey
21. White
22. Black
23. Silver
24. Sky Blue
25. Colbalt Green
26. Gold
27. Gingerbread
28. Olive
29. Turquoise
30. Peach

Key Colors:

1. Red
2. Green
3. Yellow
4. Blue
5. Orange
6. Purple
7. Cyan
8. Magenta
9. Lime
10. Pink
11. Teal
12. Lavender
13. Brown
14. Beige
15. Maroon
16. Mint
17. Olive
18. Coral
19. Navy
20. Grey
21. White
22. Black
23. Silver
24. Sky Blue
25. Colbalt Green
26. Gold
27. Gingerbread
28. Olive
29. Turquoise
30. Peach

Key Colors:

1. Red	16. Mint
2. Green	17. Olive
3. Yellow	18. Coral
4. Blue	19. Navy
5. Orange	20. Grey
6. Purple	21. White
7. Cyan	22. Black
8. Magenta	23. Silver
9. Lime	24. Sky Blue
10. Pink	25. Colbalt Green
11. Teal	26. Gold
12. Lavender	27. Gingerbread
13. Brown	28. Olive
14. Beige	29. Turquoise
15. Maroon	30. Peach

Key Colors:

1. Red
2. Green
3. Yellow
4. Blue
5. Orange
6. Purple
7. Cyan
8. Magenta
9. Lime
10. Pink
11. Teal
12. Lavender
13. Brown
14. Beige
15. Maroon
16. Mint
17. Olive
18. Coral
19. Navy
20. Grey
21. White
22. Black
23. Silver
24. Sky Blue
25. Colbalt Green
26. Gold
27. Gingerbread
28. Olive
29. Turquoise
30. Peach

Key Colors:

1. Red	16. Mint
2. Green	17. Olive
3. Yellow	18. Coral
4. Blue	19. Navy
5. Orange	20. Grey
6. Purple	21. White
7. Cyan	22. Black
8. Magenta	23. Silver
9. Lime	24. Sky Blue
10. Pink	25. Colbalt Green
11. Teal	26. Gold
12. Lavender	27. Gingerbread
13. Brown	28. Olive
14. Beige	29. Turquoise
15. Maroon	30. Peach

Key Colors:

1. Red	16. Mint
2. Green	17. Olive
3. Yellow	18. Coral
4. Blue	19. Navy
5. Orange	20. Grey
6. Purple	21. White
7. Cyan	22. Black
8. Magenta	23. Silver
9. Lime	24. Sky Blue
10. Pink	25. Colbalt Green
11. Teal	26. Gold
12. Lavender	27. Gingerbread
13. Brown	28. Olive
14. Beige	29. Turquoise
15. Maroon	30. Peach

Key Colors:

1. Red	16. Mint
2. Green	17. Olive
3. Yellow	18. Coral
4. Blue	19. Navy
5. Orange	20. Grey
6. Purple	21. White
7. Cyan	22. Black
8. Magenta	23. Silver
9. Lime	24. Sky Blue
10. Pink	25. Colbalt Green
11. Teal	26. Gold
12. Lavender	27. Gingerbread
13. Brown	28. Olive
14. Beige	29. Turquoise
15. Maroon	30. Peach

Key Colors:

1. Red
2. Green
3. Yellow
4. Blue
5. Orange
6. Purple
7. Cyan
8. Magenta
9. Lime
10. Pink
11. Teal
12. Lavender
13. Brown
14. Beige
15. Maroon
16. Mint
17. Olive
18. Coral
19. Navy
20. Grey
21. White
22. Black
23. Silver
24. Sky Blue
25. Colbalt Green
26. Gold
27. Gingerbread
28. Olive
29. Turquoise
30. Peach

Key Colors:

1. Red
2. Green
3. Yellow
4. Blue
5. Orange
6. Purple
7. Cyan
8. Magenta
9. Lime
10. Pink
11. Teal
12. Lavender
13. Brown
14. Beige
15. Maroon
16. Mint
17. Olive
18. Coral
19. Navy
20. Grey
21. White
22. Black
23. Silver
24. Sky Blue
25. Colbalt Green
26. Gold
27. Gingerbread
28. Olive
29. Turquoise
30. Peach

Key Colors:

1. Red
2. Green
3. Yellow
4. Blue
5. Orange
6. Purple
7. Cyan
8. Magenta
9. Lime
10. Pink
11. Teal
12. Lavender
13. Brown
14. Beige
15. Maroon
16. Mint
17. Olive
18. Coral
19. Navy
20. Grey
21. White
22. Black
23. Silver
24. Sky Blue
25. Colbalt Green
26. Gold
27. Gingerbread
28. Olive
29. Turquoise
30. Peach

Key Colors:

1. Red
2. Green
3. Yellow
4. Blue
5. Orange
6. Purple
7. Cyan
8. Magenta
9. Lime
10. Pink
11. Teal
12. Lavender
13. Brown
14. Beige
15. Maroon
16. Mint
17. Olive
18. Coral
19. Navy
20. Grey
21. White
22. Black
23. Silver
24. Sky Blue
25. Colbalt Green
26. Gold
27. Gingerbread
28. Olive
29. Turquoise
30. Peach

Key Colors:

1. Red
2. Green
3. Yellow
4. Blue
5. Orange
6. Purple
7. Cyan
8. Magenta
9. Lime
10. Pink
11. Teal
12. Lavender
13. Brown
14. Beige
15. Maroon
16. Mint
17. Olive
18. Coral
19. Navy
20. Grey
21. White
22. Black
23. Silver
24. Sky Blue
25. Colbalt Green
26. Gold
27. Gingerbread
28. Olive
29. Turquoise
30. Peach

Key Colors:

1. Red
2. Green
3. Yellow
4. Blue
5. Orange
6. Purple
7. Cyan
8. Magenta
9. Lime
10. Pink
11. Teal
12. Lavender
13. Brown
14. Beige
15. Maroon
16. Mint
17. Olive
18. Coral
19. Navy
20. Grey
21. White
22. Black
23. Silver
24. Sky Blue
25. Colbalt Green
26. Gold
27. Gingerbread
28. Olive
29. Turquoise
30. Peach

Key Colors:

1. Red
2. Green
3. Yellow
4. Blue
5. Orange
6. Purple
7. Cyan
8. Magenta
9. Lime
10. Pink
11. Teal
12. Lavender
13. Brown
14. Beige
15. Maroon
16. Mint
17. Olive
18. Coral
19. Navy
20. Grey
21. White
22. Black
23. Silver
24. Sky Blue
25. Colbalt Green
26. Gold
27. Gingerbread
28. Olive
29. Turquoise
30. Peach

Key Colors:

1. Red
2. Green
3. Yellow
4. Blue
5. Orange
6. Purple
7. Cyan
8. Magenta
9. Lime
10. Pink
11. Teal
12. Lavender
13. Brown
14. Beige
15. Maroon
16. Mint
17. Olive
18. Coral
19. Navy
20. Grey
21. White
22. Black
23. Silver
24. Sky Blue
25. Colbalt Green
26. Gold
27. Gingerbread
28. Olive
29. Turquoise
30. Peach

Key Colors:

1. Red
2. Green
3. Yellow
4. Blue
5. Orange
6. Purple
7. Cyan
8. Magenta
9. Lime
10. Pink
11. Teal
12. Lavender
13. Brown
14. Beige
15. Maroon
16. Mint
17. Olive
18. Coral
19. Navy
20. Grey
21. White
22. Black
23. Silver
24. Sky Blue
25. Colbalt Green
26. Gold
27. Gingerbread
28. Olive
29. Turquoise
30. Peach

Key Colors:

1. Red
2. Green
3. Yellow
4. Blue
5. Orange
6. Purple
7. Cyan
8. Magenta
9. Lime
10. Pink
11. Teal
12. Lavender
13. Brown
14. Beige
15. Maroon
16. Mint
17. Olive
18. Coral
19. Navy
20. Grey
21. White
22. Black
23. Silver
24. Sky Blue
25. Colbalt Green
26. Gold
27. Gingerbread
28. Olive
29. Turquoise
30. Peach

Key Colors:

1. Red	16. Mint
2. Green	17. Olive
3. Yellow	18. Coral
4. Blue	19. Navy
5. Orange	20. Grey
6. Purple	21. White
7. Cyan	22. Black
8. Magenta	23. Silver
9. Lime	24. Sky Blue
10. Pink	25. Colbalt Green
11. Teal	26. Gold
12. Lavender	27. Gingerbread
13. Brown	28. Olive
14. Beige	29. Turquoise
15. Maroon	30. Peach

Key Colors:

1. Red
2. Green
3. Yellow
4. Blue
5. Orange
6. Purple
7. Cyan
8. Magenta
9. Lime
10. Pink
11. Teal
12. Lavender
13. Brown
14. Beige
15. Maroon
16. Mint
17. Olive
18. Coral
19. Navy
20. Grey
21. White
22. Black
23. Silver
24. Sky Blue
25. Colbalt Green
26. Gold
27. Gingerbread
28. Olive
29. Turquoise
30. Peach

Key Colors:

1. Red	16. Mint
2. Green	17. Olive
3. Yellow	18. Coral
4. Blue	19. Navy
5. Orange	20. Grey
6. Purple	21. White
7. Cyan	22. Black
8. Magenta	23. Silver
9. Lime	24. Sky Blue
10. Pink	25. Colbalt Green
11. Teal	26. Gold
12. Lavender	27. Gingerbread
13. Brown	28. Olive
14. Beige	29. Turquoise
15. Maroon	30. Peach

Key Colors:

1. Red
2. Green
3. Yellow
4. Blue
5. Orange
6. Purple
7. Cyan
8. Magenta
9. Lime
10. Pink
11. Teal
12. Lavender
13. Brown
14. Beige
15. Maroon
16. Mint
17. Olive
18. Coral
19. Navy
20. Grey
21. White
22. Black
23. Silver
24. Sky Blue
25. Colbalt Green
26. Gold
27. Gingerbread
28. Olive
29. Turquoise
30. Peach

Key Colors:

1. Red
2. Green
3. Yellow
4. Blue
5. Orange
6. Purple
7. Cyan
8. Magenta
9. Lime
10. Pink
11. Teal
12. Lavender
13. Brown
14. Beige
15. Maroon
16. Mint
17. Olive
18. Coral
19. Navy
20. Grey
21. White
22. Black
23. Silver
24. Sky Blue
25. Colbalt Green
26. Gold
27. Gingerbread
28. Olive
29. Turquoise
30. Peach

Key Colors:

1. Red
2. Green
3. Yellow
4. Blue
5. Orange
6. Purple
7. Cyan
8. Magenta
9. Lime
10. Pink
11. Teal
12. Lavender
13. Brown
14. Beige
15. Maroon
16. Mint
17. Olive
18. Coral
19. Navy
20. Grey
21. White
22. Black
23. Silver
24. Sky Blue
25. Colbalt Green
26. Gold
27. Gingerbread
28. Olive
29. Turquoise
30. Peach

Key Colors:

1. Red
2. Green
3. Yellow
4. Blue
5. Orange
6. Purple
7. Cyan
8. Magenta
9. Lime
10. Pink
11. Teal
12. Lavender
13. Brown
14. Beige
15. Maroon

16. Mint
17. Olive
18. Coral
19. Navy
20. Grey
21. White
22. Black
23. Silver
24. Sky Blue
25. Colbalt Green
26. Gold
27. Gingerbread
28. Olive
29. Turquoise
30. Peach

Key Colors:

1. Red	16. Mint
2. Green	17. Olive
3. Yellow	18. Coral
4. Blue	19. Navy
5. Orange	20. Grey
6. Purple	21. White
7. Cyan	22. Black
8. Magenta	23. Silver
9. Lime	24. Sky Blue
10. Pink	25. Colbalt Green
11. Teal	26. Gold
12. Lavender	27. Gingerbread
13. Brown	28. Olive
14. Beige	29. Turquoise
15. Maroon	30. Peach

Key Colors:

1. Red	16. Mint
2. Green	17. Olive
3. Yellow	18. Coral
4. Blue	19. Navy
5. Orange	20. Grey
6. Purple	21. White
7. Cyan	22. Black
8. Magenta	23. Silver
9. Lime	24. Sky Blue
10. Pink	25. Colbalt Green
11. Teal	26. Gold
12. Lavender	27. Gingerbread
13. Brown	28. Olive
14. Beige	29. Turquoise
15. Maroon	30. Peach

Key Colors:

1. Red
2. Green
3. Yellow
4. Blue
5. Orange
6. Purple
7. Cyan
8. Magenta
9. Lime
10. Pink
11. Teal
12. Lavender
13. Brown
14. Beige
15. Maroon
16. Mint
17. Olive
18. Coral
19. Navy
20. Grey
21. White
22. Black
23. Silver
24. Sky Blue
25. Colbalt Green
26. Gold
27. Gingerbread
28. Olive
29. Turquoise
30. Peach

Key Colors:

1. Red
2. Green
3. Yellow
4. Blue
5. Orange
6. Purple
7. Cyan
8. Magenta
9. Lime
10. Pink
11. Teal
12. Lavender
13. Brown
14. Beige
15. Maroon
16. Mint
17. Olive
18. Coral
19. Navy
20. Grey
21. White
22. Black
23. Silver
24. Sky Blue
25. Colbalt Green
26. Gold
27. Gingerbread
28. Olive
29. Turquoise
30. Peach

Key Colors:

1. Red	16. Mint
2. Green	17. Olive
3. Yellow	18. Coral
4. Blue	19. Navy
5. Orange	20. Grey
6. Purple	21. White
7. Cyan	22. Black
8. Magenta	23. Silver
9. Lime	24. Sky Blue
10. Pink	25. Colbalt Green
11. Teal	26. Gold
12. Lavender	27. Gingerbread
13. Brown	28. Olive
14. Beige	29. Turquoise
15. Maroon	30. Peach

Key Colors:

1. Red
2. Green
3. Yellow
4. Blue
5. Orange
6. Purple
7. Cyan
8. Magenta
9. Lime
10. Pink
11. Teal
12. Lavender
13. Brown
14. Beige
15. Maroon
16. Mint
17. Olive
18. Coral
19. Navy
20. Grey
21. White
22. Black
23. Silver
24. Sky Blue
25. Colbalt Green
26. Gold
27. Gingerbread
28. Olive
29. Turquoise
30. Peach

Key Colors:

1. Red
2. Green
3. Yellow
4. Blue
5. Orange
6. Purple
7. Cyan
8. Magenta
9. Lime
10. Pink
11. Teal
12. Lavender
13. Brown
14. Beige
15. Maroon
16. Mint
17. Olive
18. Coral
19. Navy
20. Grey
21. White
22. Black
23. Silver
24. Sky Blue
25. Colbalt Green
26. Gold
27. Gingerbread
28. Olive
29. Turquoise
30. Peach

Key Colors:

1. Red
2. Green
3. Yellow
4. Blue
5. Orange
6. Purple
7. Cyan
8. Magenta
9. Lime
10. Pink
11. Teal
12. Lavender
13. Brown
14. Beige
15. Maroon
16. Mint
17. Olive
18. Coral
19. Navy
20. Grey
21. White
22. Black
23. Silver
24. Sky Blue
25. Colbalt Green
26. Gold
27. Gingerbread
28. Olive
29. Turquoise
30. Peach

Key Colors:

1. Red
2. Green
3. Yellow
4. Blue
5. Orange
6. Purple
7. Cyan
8. Magenta
9. Lime
10. Pink
11. Teal
12. Lavender
13. Brown
14. Beige
15. Maroon
16. Mint
17. Olive
18. Coral
19. Navy
20. Grey
21. White
22. Black
23. Silver
24. Sky Blue
25. Colbalt Green
26. Gold
27. Gingerbread
28. Olive
29. Turquoise
30. Peach

Key Colors:

1. Red	16. Mint
2. Green	17. Olive
3. Yellow	18. Coral
4. Blue	19. Navy
5. Orange	20. Grey
6. Purple	21. White
7. Cyan	22. Black
8. Magenta	23. Silver
9. Lime	24. Sky Blue
10. Pink	25. Colbalt Green
11. Teal	26. Gold
12. Lavender	27. Gingerbread
13. Brown	28. Olive
14. Beige	29. Turquoise
15. Maroon	30. Peach

Key Colors:

1. Red
2. Green
3. Yellow
4. Blue
5. Orange
6. Purple
7. Cyan
8. Magenta
9. Lime
10. Pink
11. Teal
12. Lavender
13. Brown
14. Beige
15. Maroon
16. Mint
17. Olive
18. Coral
19. Navy
20. Grey
21. White
22. Black
23. Silver
24. Sky Blue
25. Colbalt Green
26. Gold
27. Gingerbread
28. Olive
29. Turquoise
30. Peach

Key Colors:

1. Red
2. Green
3. Yellow
4. Blue
5. Orange
6. Purple
7. Cyan
8. Magenta
9. Lime
10. Pink
11. Teal
12. Lavender
13. Brown
14. Beige
15. Maroon
16. Mint
17. Olive
18. Coral
19. Navy
20. Grey
21. White
22. Black
23. Silver
24. Sky Blue
25. Colbalt Green
26. Gold
27. Gingerbread
28. Olive
29. Turquoise
30. Peach

BONUS!

We hope you enjoyed this coloring activity book. If you did, we would greatly appreciate hearing you feedback on *Amazon*!

Leave a review and let us know what you would like to color next! Your feedback might just inspire our next coloring book.

Made in the USA
Monee, IL
07 November 2020

46934734R00116